FEDERAL PROSE

FEDERAL PROSE

How to Write in and/or for Washington

BY

JAMES R. MASTERSON and WENDELL BROOKS PHILLIPS

Drawings by Jo Thoms

CHAPEL HILL
THE UNIVERSITY OF NORTH CAROLINA PRESS

COPYRIGHT, 1948, BY

THE UNIVERSITY OF NORTH CAROLINA PRESS

★

MANUFACTURED IN THE UNITED STATES OF AMERICA
Van Rees Press, New York

Foreword

THIS BOOK IS NOT FOR FARMERS, retailers, taxpayers, and other American citizens who must read and obey what comes from Washington. They need a book, but this is not it.

This book is for American citizens who aspire to serve their fellow men by writing the language that is written and sometimes spoken in the Nation's Capital, and thus to qualify themselves as instruments by which the power and benevolence of the Federal Government are brought to bear upon the American people.

There is no question whether the ambition to write Federal Prose is a credit to both brain and heart. But the authors of this book would not encourage false and groundless hopes, doomed only to tragic disappointment. We have therefore organized the book around six other questions:

1. Have you the courage to write Federal Prose?
2. Have you any aptitude for writing Federal Prose?
3. Can you sense the spirit of Federal Prose?
4. Can you understand the rules of Federal Prose?
5. Can you apprehend the essence of Federal Prose?
6. Could you obey an authoritative issuance couched in Federal Prose?

Each of these questions except the first is twice as hard as the one that precedes. Not more than half of our readers can answer "Yes" to the first question. Of those who do, not more than half can answer "Yes" to the second. And so on. In other words, of every sixty-four readers who begin by asking themselves the first question, as we shall present it in the first section that follows, not more than one can last to the end of the book.

We realize, indeed, that half of the readers who have followed us to this point are already too discouraged to go on. But we think it a service both to our readers and to the Federal Government to discourage all who are capable of being discouraged. We wish them well in their chosen fields of endeavor. But we dedicate this book to the tiny minority—one out of every 128—whose aspirations to write Federal Prose have any prospect of being crowned with success.

CONTENTS

	Foreword	v
I	*Have You the Courage to Write* FEDERAL PROSE?	3
II	*Have You Any Aptitude for Writing* FEDERAL PROSE?	6
III	*Can You Sense the Spirit of* FEDERAL PROSE?	9
IV	*Can You Understand the Rules of* FEDERAL PROSE?	12
V	*Can You Apprehend the Essence of* FEDERAL PROSE?	24
VI	*Could You Obey an* AUTHORITATIVE ISSUANCE *Couched in* FEDERAL PROSE?	29
	Glossary of FEDERAL PROSE *and English*	33

FEDERAL PROSE

I.

Have You the COURAGE *to Write Federal Prose?*

AT THE VERY BEGINNING you should be warned that writers of Federal Prose will find their chief reward in their own consciousness of having rendered a noble public service and in the enlightened approval of the very few Americans who can recognize the value of this service.

The service calls for a willingness to ignore the criticisms of benighted conservatism and the poisoned barbs of malicious sarcasm. The writer of Federal Prose must take for granted the ridicule, contempt, and hatred of the people he labors to serve. He must expect to be cartooned and lampooned by those who will be blind to the merit of his work. Farmers, retailers, taxpayers, and teachers of the English language

would love to burn him at the stake. Conceivably the public indignation aroused by him and his kind will sometime lead to a wholesale slaughter of the whole population of Washington.

To a noble spirit this prospect is only a challenge. Blessed are you when men shall revile you and persecute you. But they will not revile and persecute you as an individual, since they will never know that you are one.

The legal author of all that you write will be the agency that employs you, and not yourself as a legal person. Your work will be revised by other artists in Federal Prose, and in turn you will revise the work of such artists. Your most cherished phrases will be deleted, and you will delete the most cherished phrases of other authors. Probably you will never do any writing in which fewer than six other authors have had an equal part. Experience, if not intuition, will teach you the imprudence of letting your name appear on your work, and you will prefer to exist as a literary ghost.

During your uncertain and precarious life you will be obliged, like other Federal personnel, to put security above all other virtues, even to the extent of denying that you are a writer of Federal Prose. If you die a martyr, you will be an anonymous martyr, an unknown soldier of the civil service. Once dead, however, you will be safe. No one will read your work, no one will know who wrote it, and no one will care. Your literary remains will never be exhumed.

II.

Have You Any APTITUDE for Writing Federal Prose?

IF, IN SPITE OF these warnings, you persist in your ambition to serve humanity by writing Federal Prose, there is still the unhappy probability that you have no aptitude for the art. Only a select few, by the grace of an exceptional heredity and environment, possess the qualifications for acquiring a mastery of this art.

Your aptitude as a potential writer of Federal Prose can be accurately measured by the simple test that follows. Write "yes" or "no" after each question, with the possible exception of the last.

1. Are you or have you been a mathematician? _____
2. Do you like pastel shades? _____
3. Is your IQ below 130? _____
4. Can you recognize an English gerund? _____
5. Are you often amused when other people are not? _____
6. Do you like round-table discussions? _____
7. Are you in the habit of asking "Why?" _____
8. Does it embarrass you to say "I don't know"? _____
9. Are you or have you been a social worker or a sociologist? _____
10. Do you call teachers "educators"? _____
11. Did you take Spanish for credit in college? _____
12. Are you or have you been a vice president of something? _____
13. Do you like to say "no"? _____
14. Do you know two meanings for the "f" in "snafu"? _____
15. Are you an antiquarian? _____
16. Do you know what Frankie (alias Albert) did to Johnny? _____
17. Do you like to say "yes"? _____
18. Do you call a spade a spade? _____
19. Are you well rounded? _____
20. Are you in the habit of correcting other people's errors in speech? _____
21. Do you often say "Yes, but—"? _____
22. Do you pride yourself on being mentally up to date? _____
23. Do you consider yourself overpaid? _____

24. Do you write "prior to 1900" in preference to "before 1900"? _____
25. What is your usual reply to a "yes-or-no" question? _____

Grade yourself 4 points for each correct answer (answers are at the foot of this page). A score of 92 or above indicates remarkable aptitude for writing Federal Prose; 76-88, fair aptitude; 60-72, doubtful aptitude; below 60, no aptitude. If your score is below 60, you might as well stop here.

In this event, do not lose faith in yourself. Lack of aptitude for writing Federal Prose does not imply lack of aptitude for writing English or for other forms of service to humanity. Federal Prose is a rare and exalted art. If it is not for you, neither your sighs nor your tears will avail. Console yourself by finding and cultivating the talents that you do possess. Teach English; write poetry and novels; compose symphonies; paint landscapes; discover a new element or a new star; deliver mail to the right address; sell apples that are edible. To each of us some talent is given.

1. No. 2. Yes. 3. Yes. 4. No. 5. No. 6. Yes. 7. No. 8. Yes. 9. Yes. 10. Yes. 11. Yes. 12. Yes. 13. No. 14. No. 15. No. 16. No. 17. No. 18. No. 19. Yes. 20. Yes. 21. No. 22. Yes. 23. No. 24. Yes. 25. Yes and No.

III. Can You Sense the SPIRIT of Federal Prose?

IF THE TEST reveals that you have a talent for Federal Prose, you must still determine whether you can vibrate in unison with its spirit. For Federal Prose is the expression of a spirit that cannot be reduced to rules and precepts. If you do not sense this spirit, as distinctly as if it were an odor or a tune, you should transfer your ambitions to some goal other than the literary service of the Federal Government. Nothing, after all, is more common than talent. Talent for Federal Prose is not enough; the talent must be dynamic.

Your sensitiveness to this spirit can be fully tested by a single example. It is not necessary to eat all of a bad egg to know that it is bad, nor to read the entire files of the Federal Government to know that Federal Prose is good. Note the following translation from English to Federal Prose:

ENGLISH	FEDERAL PROSE
Too many cooks spoil the broth.	Undue multiplicity of personnel assigned either concurrently or consecutively to a single function involves deterioration of quality in the resultant product as compared with the product of the labor of an exact sufficiency of personnel.

Your reaction to the specimen above should be powerful and immediate. You will at once perceive the implications of the English sentence and feel concerned for the mind or minds that devised it. Who would venture to say what constitutes "too many"? Or at precisely what point anything—be it process, person, or material object—becomes "spoiled"? And why select cooks for special opprobrium? The preparation of food is an honorable occupation, and those who follow it have done nothing to deserve this notoriety. The very word "broth," moreover, is associated with witches and other antisocial personnel.

Now turn again to the concept as rendered in Federal Prose. Primitive groping is here replaced by scientific method. The precept, no longer confined to cooks, is extended to all those who labor, or, more exactly, all those who are "assigned to a function." The naïve expression "too many" is broadened to an objective comparison between "undue multiplicity" and "exact sufficiency." "Spoil," with its unsavory suggestion of babies, broth, and the Jacksonian era, gives way to the serene and factual phrase "deterioration of quality."

But why labor the point? If you are one of the chosen few, you have already felt the quiet glow of an inner consummation. This first glimpse of Federal Prose has conferred on you an apotheosis from whose height you will henceforth perceive the fugue, the pattern, the fundamental image.

IV. Can You Understand the RULES of Federal Prose?

UNFORTUNATELY THERE ARE those who respond to the spirit but who have no capacity for the unremitting labor of emmets and beavers. Such persons may as well withdraw at this point and devote themselves to the writing of minor poems.

Strictly speaking, the rules of Federal Prose may best be derived by pure induction. After examining several million cubic feet of Federal writings, even the comparatively obtuse reader will eventually understand the principles which they exhibit. But this book is addressed to beginners who have not had the privilege of such perusal. For them the following rules will serve both as a test of innate capacity and, should the ultimate goal of Federal employment be reached, as a preliminary guide for composition: *

(1) Use nouns in preference to verbs. Children, illiterates, and artists use verbs in abundance. But verbs are too direct, too outspoken, too naïve, not abstract enough to suit the needs of Federal Prose. When you are absolutely obliged to use a verb, use if possible some form of "to be," or a verb ending in "-ize," "-ate," or "-ect."

ENGLISH	FEDERAL PROSE
Time flies.	Time is fugitive. Fugacity is characteristic of time.

* See also the Glossary at the end of this volume.

ENGLISH	FEDERAL PROSE
Hens lay eggs.	Egg-laying characterizes hens. Hens are typically oviparous. Hens ovulate, though not continuously and not without exception. Gallinaceous ovulation is effected only by hens.
Jack fell down and broke his crown.	A youth designated only as "Jack" sustained, incident to a loss of equilibrium, a fracture of the cranium.

When the cat's away the mice will play.	Rodents, in the absence of their feline enemy, are prone to divert themselves.
Haste makes waste.	Precipitation entails negation of economy.
Every dog has his day.	In every canine lifespan is manifested a period of optimum euphoria.
Yours of the 20th received and contents noted.	Receipt by this office of your communication dated November 20, 1945, and cognizance of the contents thereof, are herewith acknowledged.
Please return these papers.	Return of papers is requested.

ENGLISH	FEDERAL PROSE
The old gray mare came out of the wilderness, forty-fifty years ago.	At a period subsequent to 1905 but prior to 1915 the subject mare, described as anile and in consequence grizzled, issued for motives unknown from a region defined only as uninhabited.
Man proposes but God disposes.	Human planning is subject to divine controls.

(2) Use abstract and general nouns, not concrete and particular nouns. In other words, intellectualize your nominalism. Untutored minds see particular objects. Minds trained in the Federal service see patterns and essences illustrated in particular objects.

ENGLISH	FEDERAL PROSE
Roses are red.	Rosaceae exhibit roseateness.
Scissors cut.	Scissors effect scission functionally.

Two heads are better than one.	Dual is preferred to unilateral consideration.

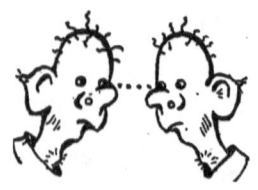

ENGLISH	FEDERAL PROSE
Call not thy brother "fool."	Avoid attribution of imbecility to your male sib.
The sun rises in the east.	Solar bodies tend to exhibit, with respect to and from the viewpoint of their satellites, an apparent orientality of anabasis.
Show your pass.	The display of your entrance permit is mandatory.
Hark! Hark! The dogs do bark. The beggars are coming to town— Some in rags, and some in tags, And some in velvet gowns.	The canine ululations now obtrusively perceptible adumbrate the visitation cityward of mendicants exhibiting a variability of costume between the extremes of quasinudity and velours. Public protests have been received with respect to the imminent concentration of artists, convicts, and doctors of philosophy in the District of Columbia.
Satisfaction guaranteed or your money back.	The remittance of sums paid by customers purchasing articles in or of this establishment is hereby guaranteed in the event that such articles, or one or more thereof, shall be hereafter deemed unsatisfactory to or by the said customers, or any of them: —provided, however, (a) that the dissatisfaction be expressed verbally or through correspondence and not otherwise, (b) that the said dissatisfaction be expressed by a customer or customers, (c) that the said customer

ENGLISH	FEDERAL PROSE
	or customers be, or have been, customers of the establishment designated hereinabove, and (d) that the said dissatisfaction relate to, and be justifiably directed toward, an article or articles purchased thereby herein.

Hey diddle diddle!
The cat and the fiddle!
  The cow jumped over the moon.
The little dog laughed
To see the sport,
  And the dish ran away with the spoon.
	The alarming because unprecedented spectacle of feline musicianship exhibited by means of catgut elicited from the spectators such reactions as, in the case of a cow, translunary saltation; of a dimunitive canine, cachinnation; and of two articles of tableware, collusive flight.

(3) Use attributive nouns in preference to adjectives or adjectival phrases.

ENGLISH	FEDERAL PROSE
The writing of books is a trade.	Book composition is a trade.
The Department of the Interior.	The Interior Department.
The search for truth is endless.	The truthquest is interminable.

(4) Avoid the rigid and unnatural parallelism of English.

ENGLISH	FEDERAL PROSE
The candidate is not only young but pretty.	The candidate not only is youthful but also personable. The candidate is not juvenile merely but is personable as well. Not only juvenile, also the candidate is personable.

ENGLISH	FEDERAL PROSE
The candidate is neither young nor pretty.	The candidate neither is youthful or is she personable.
The market will go either up or down.	In the event of its instability the market either will ascend or descend.
A candidate is wanted who can read and write.	A candidate able to read and who can write is indicated.

(5) Place clauses and phrases in such a way as to hold attention.

ENGLISH	FEDERAL PROSE
My father died when I was a baby.	When an infant my father died.
While being examined the candidate went to sleep.	In the course of examination somnolence acquired complete mastery over the candidate.

ENGLISH	FEDERAL PROSE
One rule is bad; two are worse.	One rule is bad, two worse.
Finding no weapon on Jones, the police let him go.	Finding no weapon on him, Jones was released by the police.
The chairman finds that the third report duplicated the second.	It is ascertained by the chairman the tertiary report to be duplicated by the second.

(6) Indicate explicitly the relations among all facts and ideas that you express. Do not expect your reader to solve riddles. Leave nothing to his imagination, because (*a*) he probably has none or (*b*) he may imagine something erotic. Few Federal adults can interpret the following:

> Hickory, dickory, dock.
> A mouse ran up the clock.
> The princess hopped, the fiddlers stopped,
> Not knowing what to do.

Expand this approximately as follows:

> A sound suggestive of but distinguishable from striking issued from a tall clock in a ballroom in which a princess was but the most distinguished of the gay multitude that whirled in unison to the strains of a corps of violinists. Startled by the sudden and discordant plangency, the beauteous scion of royalty stumbled to an abrupt halt in her graceful evolutions; the orchestra, confused by this cessation of movement, subsided into silence; and only after investigation had divulged the origin of the perturbing phenomena in the hitherto unsuspected ascent, within the clock, of a rodent that had in some manner not ascertained effected adit thereto, were the festivities resumed.

Figurative language (unless two or more figures are combined) is inappropriate to the Federal service. The following proverb would not be readily understood:

> Though thou shouldest bray a fool in a mortar among wheat with a pestle, yet will not his foolishness depart from him.

This could be rewritten for Federal purposes somewhat as follows:

> All efforts looking toward alteration induced from without of the congenital mental configuration of personnel are ill advised, adaptation of administrative methodology thereto in contradistinction to adaptation thereof to administrative methodology being indicated.

(7) When using words that are in dictionaries, use them in senses that are unknown to lexicographers. Employ either *synecdoche* (designation of part as whole or of whole as part) or *transference* (migration of meaning from a word to another word often found in the same context).

Classified documents; i.e., documents classified as restricted, confidential, secret, or top secret. (Non-Federal readers, coming upon this phrase, will suppose that it refers to documents that are arranged by a system of classification, as distinguished from documents not so arranged. In view of the nature of classified documents, it is well that they should be designated somewhat mysteriously, so that the general public will think that it knows what it does not know. If it knew that it cannot see the documents, it would want to see them.)

Document file; i.e., a file consisting of folded papers as distinguished from one consisting of flat or bound papers. (Here, again, non-Federal readers will suppose that they know what they do not know. They will assume that a document file is a file consisting of documents, as distinguished from a file consisting of something that is not documents. Not knowing that other files also consist of documents, they will not care to see those files.)

Higher or lower *echelons* of command. (Formerly, echelons were units of a body of troops, each, except the last, drawn up parallel to but to right or left of the unit in its rear. All the units were characterized by being at different distances from the officer in command. Levels of command in the hierarchy of army organization have this same characteristic. The mathematical line extending from an officer to an echelon is horizontal; the metaphysical line extending from an officer to his superior or subordinate is vertical; the two lines are at right angles to each other, forming a Greek cross of which the orientation is inconsequential and, if insisted on, would occasion intellectual strain.)

Inhabitants *evacuated* from a town. (Etymologically, to evacuate is to cause to be vacant or empty. A town is evacuated when it is caused to be vacant. Its inhabitants are evacuated when they are caused to be empty, as by catharsis or fright. The inhabitants can evacuate the town by leaving it. Military authorities can evacuate the town either by departing from it themselves or by causing the inhabitants to depart from it. In the latter event, the inhabitants are removed from the town. The removal of the inhabitants is equated with the evacuation of the town. Therefore evacuation is the same as removal. Therefore the inhabitants are evacuated from the town and are designated as evacuees.)

(8) Learn to punctuate scientifically.

a. Federal prose is not subject to the trivial rules of English punctuation, which were designed by pedants for the needless discomfiture of the young. The concepts of punctuation in Federal Prose are larger and broader than those entertained by novelists, poets, and scholars. They follow the principle of *flexibility of interpretation* explained in Section V below.

b. When tempted to punctuate, first ask "Is it necessary?" Though use of a period at the end of a sentence is often allowable, even this can generally be avoided by a skillful grouping into sections, subsections, and sub-subsections, each with its proper symbol of designation and with the required degree of indentation.

c. Never use commas recklessly. The attempt to make a sentence clear on first reading is a juvenile practice that should be avoided.

ENGLISH	FEDERAL PROSE
Tom, Dick, and Harry went down the street.	Tom, Dick and Harry went down the street. (It is unnecessary to inquire whether the three persons mentioned went down the street, or whether Tom is being told that the other two did so. Even teachers and journalists are discarding use of the comma between the last two members of a series—and to this extent, English and Federal Prose are becoming ONE.)

| The superintendent ordered the children to burn all waste paper, and teachers saw that the order was carried out. | The superintendent ordered the children to burn all waste paper and teachers saw that the order was carried out. (A comma in this sentence would insult the reader's intelligence.) |

d. Use semicolons only under extreme duress. Any person whose thought-pattern includes the semicolon is not qualified to write Federal Prose. Typists are cautioned, however, not to remove this symbol from their machines (though the type-bar could be utilized for some more serviceable mark), since a few old-fashioned office chiefs insist on using semicolons in their letters to Congressmen.

e. The colon, on the other hand, is indispensable in Federal Prose, since it has become the great symbol of anticipation and logical order. There is, indeed, some question whether the Federal Government could operate without it. Skillfully used, it reveals the master, particularly in breaking the backbone of a stubborn sentence. Amateurish: "His favorite colors were red, green, and blue." Competent: "His favorite colors were: red, green and blue." Professional:

His favorite colors were:
  I. red
  II. green
  III. blue
  IV. or, a combination of the three above colors, with:
      A. red predominating
      B. green predominating
      C. blue predominating
      D. or, a balanced combination of the foregoing colors in which none of the following predominates:
          (x) red
          (y) green
          (z) blue

V

Can You Apprehend the ESSENCE of Federal Prose?

I*f* you have arrived at this point, you are one of four survivors out of the 128 readers who read the first sentence of the foreword of this book. You have proved that you have eyes and ears. You must now prove that you have brains.

You must already have perceived that all the rules and all the examples presented above are variations and illustrations of a single cardinal rule:

Always write in a style that can be interpreted flexibly.

Not only the rule but its explanation are almost undoubtedly apparent to you. The Federal Government is a government of limited powers, set forth in the Constitution of 1789, in the amendments to the Constitution, and in the acts of Congress and the decisions of the Supreme Court. All powers not granted to the Federal Government are presumed to be retained by the several States and by the citizens of the United States. But ever since 1789 the Federal Government has found itself in a state of chronic emergency, requiring freedom to act or to be inactive at each moment as circumstances might dictate. The solution has been achieved in the development of a form of language that is always susceptible of several interpretations. This is Federal Prose.*

Federal Prose is that form of nonmetrical composition, apparently English, which can be invariably interpreted as meaning and/or not meaning more and/or less than, rather than what, it seems to mean.

Without this implement the Federal Government could never have come into existence, and the Constitution of 1789 could never have been written. Complete clarity and precision of language would have doomed the American Nation and each of its States to an unwritten constitution and to oral statutes.

Let us examine the matter more closely. It is obvious that Federal Prose is the only instrument possessing all the following advantages, each of which is indispensable to the operations of the Federal Government:

---

* The President of the United States, because of his special relation to the public, is permitted, though not required, to write English. The privilege is sometimes exercised, also, by members of the Cabinet and justices of the Supreme Court.

(1) Federal Prose permits compromise, each party to which finds in the phraseology of the instrument of compromise a frame of language that seems to convey the meaning desired by each.

(2) It permits the Federal Government to exercise powers that were not known to be conveyed by the instrument of authorization, and to refrain from the exercise of powers that were thought to be conveyed thereby.

(3) It permits supervisors to rebuke subordinates for what can be represented either as arrogation of powers not conveyed by the instrument of authorization or as dereliction of duties therein enjoined.

(4) It permits subordinates in this contingency to defend their action or inaction by a different interpretation of the same instruments.

(5) It permits all concerned, in response to changing conditions, to vary and alter the extent and character of administrative action through reinterpretation of the instrument of authorization, which itself remains unchanged.

(6) It permits both the alert and the inattentive, both the percipient and the imperceptive, to find in language what they need to find, the former being assured that they do not know what they know and the latter being assured that they know what they do not know.

(7) It permits the linguistic basis of administration to be infused with an infinite variety that time cannot wither nor custom stale; but the more it changes, the more it is the same thing;—and thus it solves, in democratic terms, the problem of the one and the many.

No doubt a suspicion has dawned that Federal Prose is not a dialect of English. We in the United States have (1) the Western Dialect, otherwise known as General American, spoken by about three fourths of the American people, (2) the Southern Dialect, heard more often than any other in the Nation's Capital, (3) the New England Dialect, and (4) the Brooklyn Dialect;—but, in strict accuracy, there is no Potomac Dialect. Nobody ever grew up speaking naturally the language of the Federal Government. Even the children who are constantly being bred and born in the District of Columbia and in the adjacent counties of Maryland and Virginia have no spontaneous command of this language. Most of them could never, by any conceivable effort, even if they should live a thousand years, make themselves masters of it.

"Federal Prose" as a designation for the language of Washington is itself, by synecdoche, an example of Federal Prose, which is by no means confined to the use of the Federal Government. It occurs in various other products of semantic art:—in the writings and oral utterances of sociologists and educators, in the iridescent commentaries of theologians, in the texts of insurance policies, in reviews of plays and concerts, in advertisements of motor vehicles, novels, and tomato soup.

Experience in any of these linguistic provinces is a useful preparation for the linguistic service of the Federal Government. Conversely, the worst possible preparation for this service is to have studied, or still more to have taught, a language or a natural (i.e., not a social) science. Even under these handicaps a candidate may find some utility in his experience with the exposition of Riemann's space or with the analysis of pneumatic soteriology; and a candidate trained in metaphysics may acclimate himself to the Federal service by adopting tentatively any of the current forms of monodualisticpluralistic eclecticism.

Even so, the purist and the precisian, whether in or out of the Federal service, will probably feel vaguely dissatisfied with the term "Federal Prose." Some years ago a gifted Texan, then in the Federal service, coined the name "Gobbledegook," which suggested itself because of a resemblance between the language of Washington and the language of turkeys.

The sounds made by turkeys, however, are not articulate and therefore are not capable of developing into written form and becoming a medium of Federal communication. Perhaps they could be reduced to some simple style of musical notation, conveying without ambiguity, even to readers experienced in the ways of Federal Prose, whatever a turkey might desire to convey—faith, hope, charity, temperance, prudence, justice, fortitude, pride, envy, wrath, sloth, avarice, gluttony, lechery. These things cannot be expressed in Federal Prose, which is not meleagrine but psittacine. In the South, moreover, "Gobbledegook" is reported to imply a certain lack of virility. Hence the term has been reluctantly laid aside.

VI

Could You Obey an AUTHORITATIVE ISSUANCE of Federal Prose?

THIS BRIEF, LAST section is addressed to the two readers out of 128 who have survived the five tests, screens, or sieves that precede. One of the two readers will be eliminated. Both are invited to scrutinize the following directive:

Bureau of Lost Ships
Widows & Orphans of Captains
Insurance Branch
Step-Childrens' Claims Section

Authoritative Issuance 001-xxvi
Subject: Fiscal Year-End Language Shift
Object: Anticipation of Budget Bureau Requirements
Concerning Personnel Language Competence

Recent rapid turnover of typists and editorial supervisors in this Unit (if in doubt as to unit of reference see lines 1-4 above) has eventuated in a degree of drop in the language-competence curve such that concern is felt on the policy making levels. Full realization being had of the necessity of reversing this curve-trend to a direction more nearly approximating the upward-vertical, suggestions are:

1. Aim: Language Competence
2. Competency Attainment Means:

(a) Numerous newly inducted personnel of the several Government agencies are handicapped in their initial mastery of Federal Prose by a knowledge of English habituated prior to their induction. Until a program for personnel induction at the infant level can be coordinated with the Federal Prose tutorship objectives, this situation will continue to create embarrassments at the administrative and higher levels. Only drastic and immediate action will achieve the impact on the linguistic functions involved necessary and liquidate a stylistic status recognized as inoperable.

(b) At the risk of and aware of the contingency by which personnel morale might be undermined, it is hereby urged that personnel cease contacting the outmoded English language verbally and/or orally, and that they terminate all sponsorship thereof as of 30 June of the current fiscal year.

(c) Pending the report of the Committee on Inquiry acting as subsidiary to the Phonological Unit, this quasi-nonmandatory shift must for the major part be a self-help extra-budgetary project. However, it is felt that earnest inductees should be supplied and supplemented with a procedural data file on which emergency efforts at the preliminary echelon in the Federal Prose mastery field may be posited and by which their semi-involuntary detachment from addiction to superseded English phraseology may be effectuated with a maximum utilization of established techniques and a minimum cancelation of man- and/or woman-hours.

(d) It is believed that the herewith attached manual * will serve roughly to channelize typists and build up the outstanding desired attitudes in scriptatory personnel. Approved by the Federal Prose Establishment Board, it is pursuantly offered with a view to consummating quick idiom-shifts from the crude vernacular into forms certified as acceptable.

* * * *

The sole surviving reader of this book is he who discovers that in his own writing he has been strictly obedient to this directive without knowing that it had been issued—obedient because it formalizes all the practices which for him are not an art and a science to be acquired by imitation and discipline, but a spontaneous expression of his real nature.

In other words, Gentle Reader, you must now realize that you have been writing Federal Prose without knowing it.

* *Federal Prose: How to Write in and/or for Washington*, by James R. Masterson (Ph.D.) and Wendell Brooks Phillips (M.A.). File clerks should note that this manual (now being referred to) constitutes Inclosure A to this (now being read) authoritative issuance, and that this authoritative issuance constitutes an insertion under Section VI of the manual. File accordingly.

BLS-CW&OIB-S/CCS-4/19/46

Glossary

ENGLISH	FEDERAL PROSE
ABOUT (prep.)	Prefer *relating to, respecting, with respect to, concerning, regarding, vis a vis*. To distinguish among these expressions except for elegant variation is a form of purism now obsolete. For *about* in the sense of *approximately* substitute *around:* "Around 1851."
ADVOCATE (n.)	Prefer *protagonist*, as antonym of *antagonist*.
AFTER	With reference to time, prefer *subsequent to:* "The undersigned will be pleased to discuss the matter with you subsequent to lunch." *Following* is also recommended: "Following his marriage he gained weight." For variety use *posterior to* or *pursuant to*.
BECAUSE OF	Prefer *due to* in adverbial uses: "Due to a cold the speaker sneezed" (better, *sternutated*). *Because of* is permissible in adjectival uses: "The speaker's sternutation was because of a respiratory condition."

ENGLISH	FEDERAL PROSE
BEFORE	Avoid this childlike lapse into English by always using *prior to* in chronological relations: "I will be unable to contact you prior to tomorrow." Additional dignity may be had by substituting *anterior to:* "He was separated from the service 3 days anterior to his decease."
BIRTH CONTROL	Unless a facetious effect is intended, prefer *spaced parenthood.*
BUREAUCRACY	Always substitute *administrative democracy* for the vicious vulgarism listed in the opposite column.
BUT	Prefer *however:* "This factor is meaningful, however it is not the basic element in the problem."
CASE	To be avoided with respect to containers. Wrong: "A case of beer and a box of books." Right: "2 containers of beer and books respectively." *Case* is admirable with respect to situations. Wrong: "Mrs. X underwent an operation for tumor." Right: "A tumor was excised in Mrs. X's case." Wrong: "The dog is dead." Right: "In the case of the dog demise has occurred."
CLASS (n.)	Prefer *category*, as would Kant and Aristotle: "Members of the white-collar category are insufficiently remunerated."
COMPOSED OF	Prefer *comprised of:* "The program was comprised of three lectures." In this instance

ENGLISH	FEDERAL PROSE
	comprised is particularly appropriate if the program contained not only lectures but something else, such as motion pictures.
CONNECTED WITH, RESULTING FROM	Prefer *incident to:* "Sternutation is incident to respiratory conditions."
CONSENSUS	Used only when followed by *of opinion*. Preferred spelling: *concensus*. Eventual prescription of this spelling, in spite of etymological objections, may be confidently anticipated. For variation use *climate of opinion*.
COMBINE, UNITE	Prefer *consolidate* or *integrate*, which should be used both interchangeably and frequently.
CRIMINAL (n.)	Translate as *public enemy*.
DESTRUCTION	Prefer *liquidation*. "Conflagration effected the liquidation of the edifice."
DISCHARGE	Never used in referring to loss of a job; substitute *involuntary separation*.
DIVERSIFIED	The established locution is *well-rounded*, better written *wellrounded*. The circle and the sphere are obviously the noblest of geometric forms. "In Heaven the perfect round."
DO	Whenever possible, substitute *effect*, which should occur not fewer than three times on each page.
DOUBLE	Prefer *duplex*

ENGLISH	FEDERAL PROSE
DUTY	*Function* should be substituted for *duty, habit, characteristic, operation,* or any other word about which the writer is in doubt. The word must occur at least five times to the page.
EFFECT, INFLUENCE (n.)	*Impact* is more scientific, and at the same time more dramatic, dynamic, and challenging.
EMPLOYEES	Always substitute *personnel*.
EXCELLENT	Use *worthwhile* or *outstanding*. Never attempt fine distinctions in meaning by the use of such outmoded words as *prominent, distinguished, chief, superior, conspicuous, eminent,* or *valuable;* to do so is sheer pedantry, contrary to the spirit of Federal Prose.
FIRST WORLD WAR, SECOND WORLD WAR	Translate as *World War I, World War II.* This usage, now mandatory in Federal agencies, is so effective that it is bound to set a pattern. Trite: "The Smith baby has cut its first tooth." Better: "In the alveolar tissue of the Smith infant's oral orifice has transpired the emergence of Tooth I."
FOREGOING, PRECEDING	Superseded in official correspondence by *above:* "The above data."
FUNDAMENTAL	Debarred by obscene connotations; substitute *basic* or *foundation:* "The basic elements; the foundation principles." *Elemental* is also recommended: "The elemental bases."
GENERAL (adj.)	Prefer *overall* (no hyphen).

ENGLISH	FEDERAL PROSE
GET	Make no attempt to distinguish between *get* (obtain) and *have* (possess); always use the passive voice: "Butter may be had in limited amounts."
I, WE	These expressions offend in both their egotism and their suggestion of unsocialized orientation. Substitute either *the undersigned* or a passive construction: "The undersigned seizes upon the opportunity of conveying to Your Honor the assurance of his distinguished consideration." "Appreciation is desired to be expressed for the permission granted in your communication of the 17th inst."
IMPLEMENT	When a noun is desired, substitute *adjunct* or *agency:* "A rake is a worthwhile adjunct to raking leaves." Permissible as a verb: "The execution was implemented by lethal gas."
IMPORTANT	Prefer *vital*.
IN	Properly confined to metaphorical uses. Wrong: "The cat is in the basement." Right: "The location of the cat in question has been determined as the basement of the edifice involved." Right: "The societary impact of *cimex lectularius* is in William X. Smith, *Social Entomology in Its Teleological Aspects*."
INFORM	Substitute *advise:* "Smith advised the undersigned he nonconcurred in the projected policy." *Inform* may be used in the sense of

37

ENGLISH	FEDERAL PROSE
	delate: "His function was to inform the FBI concerning rum-smuggling offenders."
INFORMATION, FACTS	Prefer *data* (always singular): "This data is outstanding."
INTERVAL	Translate as either *hiatus* or *interim*.
INVESTIGATE	In reference to a problem, prefer *explore*.
IRRELEVANT	Prefer *tangential*.
LATTER	Correctly used only with regard to the most adjacent of three or more referents: "Tom, Dick, and Harry are sibs. The latter is the oldest."
LETTERS	Prefer *correspondence*.
LEVEL	Permissible in all senses that have become current since the earlier publications of Freud, but not in any previous sense: "At the childhood level humans like candy."
MAKE	Current colloquially among adolescents. Prefer *create:* "Mrs. Smith is creating a batch of doughnuts." Also prefer *create* to *establish:* "This Bureau was created to cope with insects."
MENTAL, EMOTIONAL	Outmoded adjectives, the referents of which do not exist. Substitute *psychological* or, better, *psychic*.
MILK (n.)	Always requires restriction by an adjective: "Fluid milk" (that is, milk that is either a

ENGLISH	FEDERAL PROSE
	liquid or a vapor, as distinguished from solid milk).
MODERATE	Tolerated only in the usage of the Weather Bureau. Substitute *conservative:* "A conservative estimate" (an estimate neither high nor low).
MONEY	Avoided in polite society; prefer *funds, finances, units of currency,* even if the reference is to $0.05.
-NESS, -ING, -TH	These suffixes are confined to colloquial use. Prefer *-ion, -tude, -ence, -ance, -ure, -ity.* Wrong: "The width of the building; sureness of touch." Right: "The extension of the structure; certitude of taction." Emulate such models as the following: "The current linguistic situation, if not the initiation of the termination, is the termination of the initiation. The reorganization of verbal expression constitutes a function of public administration incident to the obligation of liquidation of the social separations that hamper communication on both the nationwide and the ecumenical level."
NOT ONLY BUT ALSO	Highly desirable when the construction immediately following *but also* differs in grammatical nature from that following *not only.* Wrong: "The author of this list is not only an ignoramus but a pedant." Right: "This list's author not only is an ignoramus but a pedant."

ENGLISH	FEDERAL PROSE
	Right: "The evacuees resisted not only the guard but they also liquidated him."
OF	Never to be used as part of the title of an agency or administrative unit. Wrong: "The minutes of the Board on Investigation of Potentialities of Instrumentalities Looking toward the Liquidation of Noxious Reptilians in the Mountains of the Moon." Right: "The Moon Mountains Noxious Reptilians Liquidation Instrumentalities Investigation Board minutes," or, for typist-hour economy, "The MMNRLIIB minutes." In all other contexts, when possible, attributive nouns are to be substituted for adjectival prepositional phrases. Bad: "The study of history." Good: "History study."
ONLY	Prolepsis is invariably incident to the correct placement of this adverb. Wrong: "I withdraw my objections only because of your inability to understand them." Right: "The objections of the undersigned are only withdrawn due to your psychological impermeability to the application of all feasible techniques of exposition."
OPINION, RESPONSE	Substitute *reaction* for both.
OR	Less exact than *and/or*. Bad: "Smith lives in Centerville or Middletown" (ignores the probability that he has a winter residence in one and a summer home in the other, or an apart-

40

ENGLISH	FEDERAL PROSE
	ment in each incident to a state of diversified domesticity).
ORAL	Now tolerated only in medical usage: "Oral hygiene." Right: "A verbal agreement" (words are always spoken; so-called "words" in print or manuscript are only symbols of words).
PART	Prefer *portion* (except for aliquot parts).
PARTLY, IN PART	Prefer *partially*.
PROBABLE	Obsolescent for *probative*, though substitution of the latter has not yet surmounted the toryism of lexicographers.
PROVOCATIVE	Correctly used wherever no obscene implication is intended, and particularly as a modifier of *discussion, panel, forum*, and the like.
PURPOSE	Always prefer *objective*. Wrong: "His purpose was to simplify the work of the office." Right: "His objective was office technique simplification."
QUANTITY, NUMBER	The more flexible word *amount* should be used wherever possible. Bad: "Such a large quantity of records could not be stored in the building." Good: "The amount of Government documents in Washington is approaching 15 billion cu. ft." Desirable: "The amount of men in the boat was sufficient to sink same."

ENGLISH	FEDERAL PROSE
RED TAPE	Substitute *through channels*. Unpardonable: "Red tape is the curse of Government work." Correct: "Regularization of procedure through channels is conducive to uniformity of product, distribution of responsibility, and nonabruptness of terminability."
REPAIR, RESTORE	Prefer *rehabilitate*. Wrong: "To repair the porch of one's house." Right: "To rehabilitate by means of the application of paint to exposed surfaces and/or the replacement of deteriorated deals the porch of one's domicile."
SAFE, SAFETY	Prefer *secure, security,* which have become key words in progressive administration.
SAY	A vulgarism; substitute *state:* "In response to Jack's query, Jane stated in the affirmative."
SEEM	Dialectal and colloquial for *appear*. Bad: "Things are not what they seem." Good: "Entities are not what they appear to be."
SEEM NECESSARY	Substitute the appropriate form of *indicate*. Wrong: "Removal of the eyeball seems necessary." Right: "Enucleation is indicated."
SITUATION	Usually designated as *picture:* "The committee gets the picture from this memo."
START, BEGIN	Prefer *initiate*.
STATE, CONDITION	Prefer *status*. Wrong: "Sugar is hard to get in time of war." Right: "The wartime status of sugar is quasiunobtainable." Wrong: "The

ENGLISH	FEDERAL PROSE
	prisoner was drunk." Right: "The prisoner's status was alcoholic."
SUBJECT, PROFESSION	Translate as *field*. Correct: "The field of discussion; the sociology field; a field of specialization. What is your field? The teaching field is understaffed." The term *field* applies also to any physical location outside the city of Washington: "The Bureau Chief made a trip to the field." "The picture in the field was one of regrettable Government records maltreatment, notably basement storage and other practices conducive to fungoid, insectoid, and rodentoid deterioration."
SUBMARINE (n.)	Translate as *underwater element*.
SUITABLE	Prefer *idoneous*.
SUPERSEDE	Reformed spelling *supercede,* to reduce expenditures for the purchase of erasers in administrative offices.
TEACHER	Archaic except as an expression of deserved opprobrium. Prefer *educator* or better, *educationist*. Cf. *mortician, realtor*.
THAT (conj.)	Correctly used only to introduce a noun clause that begins a sentence: "That the Semantics Branch, Effectiveness Division, Communication Bureau has cognizance of the functions brought into question pending reorganization is obvious." In any other position the omission

ENGLISH	FEDERAL PROSE
	of conjunctival *that* is obligatory: "Mayor Jones advised Alderman Smith roaches were prevalent in downtown cafeterias."
THING	Entirely obsolete; translate as *entity*.
THIS	Correctly used as a demonstrative pronoun only if no explicit antecedent (noun, noun clause, infinitive) is present: "The Committee failed to meet. This was why no report was submitted."
UNUSUAL, EXCEPTIONAL	Prefer *unique:* "The most unique star in a galaxy of outstanding personnel."
UNTIL	When possible, substitute *pending*. Wrong: "Discussion will be postponed until you arrive." Right: "Discussion will be deferred pending your arrival."
USE (v.)	Prefer *utilize* because of its trisyllabic rhythm.

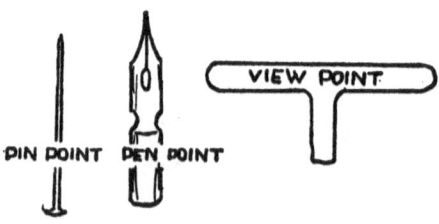

VIEW, POINT OF VIEW	Current only among niggling pedants and querulous tories. Substitute *viewpoint*. Unlike other kinds of points, viewpoints should be broad. Good: "Your viewpoints are too narrow."

ENGLISH	FEDERAL PROSE
WHETHER	Space can always be saved by using *if*. Translate English *if* as *in the event that*.
WHICH	Permissible only after a comma; otherwise use *that*.
WHILE	Correctly used only as a variant of *though*. The implication of concurrent duration that purists find in *while* is properly conveyed by *coincident with:* "Nero operated a violin coincident with the combustion of Rome."
WILD ANIMALS, BIRDS, FISH, POISON IVY	Substitute *wildlife*.

www.ingramcontent.com/pod-product-compliance
Lightning Source LLC
Chambersburg PA
CBHW031715230426
43668CB00006B/224